C.M.Brophy

DUMB, FUCKED and BLIND

PLAY SCRIPT for live theatre

by

C.M.Brophy

DUMB, FUCKED and BLIND

Playscript for theatre

by

C.M.Brophy

This play is dedicated to Dude Theatre's founding members, all our collaborators and audiences, 30 years late.

Brophy Amalgamated Publishing

4703 Banner st. Hyattsville, MD. U.S.A. 20781 (301) 785-9626

brophypublishing@gmail.com

DUMB, FUCKED and BLIND

Dramatis personae:

Marcus Shepard: 58, Bethesda MD. Tenured humanities professor, the actual bulk of his duties are administrative as assistant chair, perennial interim second banana. A polite and thoughtful man whose infrequent sardonic jokes simply kill, the contrast between speaker and content being so complete. Looks like a scientist, trim as an astronaut, conservatively old fashioned in dress and grooming, horn rimmed eyeglasses. Smiling bright eyes. Drinks Gin. Married to-

Ruth Shepard: 58, Volunteer webmaster jane for a non profit organization, she has no lady friends, but attends many Washington D.C. area meetings, marches, protests, fundraisers, rallies, and performances. Dull -sexless -righteous. Teetotaler. Vegan. Correct on all issues. Socially crippled by her distinctive nervous behaviors. Hysterical and gluten free- mother of-

Thomas Shepherd: 26, Tall, offensively good looking, beautiful table manners. Soft spoken like his father, also like his father, his eyeglasses strengthen his face. A swell cut of the jaw, well put together. Classical violinist musician post grad student. An eerie listener. A prude. Older brother to-

Sophia Shepherd: 17, A.K.A., Sophie, Lil'-bit or Sissy. The quintessential troubled teenaged younger sister. Sex, drugs and whatever passes for rock and roll rebellion, youthfully manic depressive. Drawn to extreme fashion choices. Damaged by privilege. Substance enthusiast. Rewarded for mederotricorty since birth. Love starved. Gravity defying.

Sam Ford: 58, from Santa Cruz, Ca. Built like a bear, surfer gone to seed, never worn a necktie. Owns the beach town Irish-y literary (sort of) pub, The Poetic Plough, thinks he's Ernest Hemingway, drinks a lot of whiskey, beer and wine and smokes a lot of cigars and marijuana. Has that extended mid-life crisis, pre heart attack dauntlessness. Coupled-up with but never married to-

Rebbie Granger: 39, again. California dreamer, runs a farmers market, does tarot readings, yoga instructor, artistic, surfer, attractively healthy bicycle hippy, a sunburnt leather skinned knockout of a certain age. Sensualy, sexualy and spiritually vehement. Well traveled. Interests include but are not limited to witches, wiccans, druids, native americans, voodoo, santeria, buddhism, daoist, taoist, psychedelic drugs, feminism, early Gay rights activist. Thinks today's L.G.B.T. young people are noodling fairies who enjoy what they've not earned. An omnivore, gourmet and wine connoisseur. Mother with Sam to-

Becky Granger-Ford: 25, Engaged and then married to Thomas. She's a scientist at U.M.D. grad student in Medical imaging technologies, Scary smart, mature, beautiful, success story in waiting whose sociological judgements are a mystery, childhood friends with-

Sheldon Downs: 27, a wealthy West Side Manhattan artist, very stylish, is the epitome of what used to be called a screaming homosexual except he inhabits a world where the gay lifestyle enhances professionally his status and success. Wickedly intelligent, verbose, amoral and well read.

The Survivalist: Played by the Sheldon or Thomas actor

The Inquisitor: Played by the Sheldon actor

Setting and stage properties:

Up stage a cyclorama for natural sky and clouds projections. Just downstage of the cyc is a concentric semi circular bamboo geometric lattice work. The playing area consists of a platform covered in tatami mats, japanese single story facade with sliding shoji screens, three steps down to a pebble garden with large rock island, a porch wing doubles as a raft, Bunraku or Kabuki style trap doors and windows and cabinet works, however there's no reference to asian culture in any other aspects of the performance.

Scenes

Act 1: Engagement party   at Thomas and Becky's D.C. apartment

Act 2: Wedding party   at a Georgetown hotel

Act 3: The River   beautiful cumulonimbus May above the Chesapeake watershed, natural morphing play of light shadow/ blues/ whites/ greys/ sunsets/ dawns and midnights, moonlight stark, even tule fog-mists and drizzles to deluge effects... The weather is a character.

Act 4: Inquiry   a room in a civic or professional building

ACT 1

Engagement party at Thomas and Becky's D.C. Apartment- dumb show with music and vignettes depicting guests leaving a party- only family & Sheldon remain as house lights fall.

SISSY: Daddy, no.

MARCUS: What?

SISSY: Nothing.

MARCUS: Nothing, nothing, you were going to stop me drinking from your cup weren't you?

SISSY: That's not my cup.

MARCUS: Oh really? *(Marcus drinks)*... Bleech! Sophie! It's half rum, and what? Hawaiian Punch? Oh Sissy, no it's yours alright, who else but a teeny bopper would mix such a high octane cocktail with hawaiian punch?

SISSY: I dunno', a homoserxual maybe, it's not mine Da.

MARCUS: Then why were you trying to keep me from tasting it? Huh, smarty girl? Ha.

SISSY: Because-

MARCUS: Because why darling?

SISSY: Because I didn't want you to catch me.

MARCUS: Un-huh, I thought so-

SISSY: Catch me smoking.

MARCUS: You don't smoke.

SISSY: I don't drink either, but there you go. Daddy, stop drinking that, there's a cigarette butt in it!

MARCUS: (*pause*) I know... (*stretches jaw*) Smokey.

SISSY: You know, you are funny. Ha ha daddy, you are such an idiot.

MARCUS: I love you sweetheart.

SISSY: I love you Da.

MARCUS: Don't drink and smoke sweetheart, your mother will have conniptions.

SISSY: OK, I won't, not here where she'll see.

MARCUS: Not here, where she'll see, she'll have conniptions.

SISSY: What are conniptions? I've been ignoring that word for years.

MARCUS: Ignoring "conniptions", for years? Why didn't you look it up? Who else says Conniptions?

SISSY: Nobody says it but you and Granmum-mum, I was hoping it would just go away, what does it even mean?

MARCUS: Conniption? A fit of hysterical rage, conniption.

SISSY: Like Mom has every other day.

MARCUS: If only, those still waters run too deep, a little primal scream therapy might do a world of good... *(Sheldon has entered and overheard the last part)*

SHELDON: A little spinal creaming would do the world some good alrighty, *(he screams, extends hand towards Marcus)*- Sheldon. Sheldon Downs, I'm childhood friends with the blushing bride to be, you're the groom's father right, you must be, such handsome men in your family. Cheekbones for days, is that my drink, ewww, Grody to the max, somebody put out their butt in my Strawberry Tarantula, I'm calling child services.

MARCUS: Marcus Shepard, yes Thomas' father, guilty, and this is my daughter, Sophia.

SISSY: Strawberry Tarantula, wild, is that Hawaiian punch?

SHELDON: Strawberry snapple and bacardi 151, oh you're cute, I need to meet mom, is your mommy here dear, come-come, introduce me, you have very beautiful children Mr. Shepherd, an embarrassment of riches.

SISSY: Oh-Oh, Sheldon, are you the artist?

SHELDON: I am, I am The artist, did you see the inside of the closet? I did that, get it? Ta-Ta daddy. *(Sheldon taking Sophia away)* Do you smoke Hashish? It gives me the fear but Jon Louis left me some, it's from Morocco, I heard you can see the indian on the capitol from the roof, the view is nothing compared to Manhattan where I live now, but you have to get outdoors in the summer here, D.C. is like a turkish bath, so muggy don't you think... *(Sheldon and Sissy Exit)*...

Later at the same party after further drinking

SHELDON: I finally found a real friend, a pet to call my own, isn't she darling, my soul mate, this little girl has such grace, oh Sophie girl, you are such a clumsy puppy. I just love you, don't you just love her; she calls me Shelley- I always wanted to be called Shelley, like Shelley Winters, even from when I was a child. But Daddy would've killed me. No really Lil'Bit. Lit-er-at-ly. Bang-bang. (*exits for a new bottle of prosecco*)

SISSY: Really?! No. Shelley's father would have killed him? With a gun? (*The others answer by not* answering.) He would've shot his own baby faggot son? That's Terrible.

REBBIE: It was a different world not too long ago, the race riots were here, like right out the window, when, late right? Like the 70's right, this was a Jim Crow town not too very long ago, in the shadow of the Lincoln memorial. The top of the south.

SAM: The mason dixon line's north of here, this sticky heat is awful, how do you guys cope?

MARCUS: Air Conditioning.

BECKY: That generation, Sheldon's parents, our parents, the end of the baby boomers, they are all insane. Different crazy, your folks and my folks, quite different seemingly, and Sheldon's parents- Whoo-ee, but all of em, crazy, shock therapy had it's place in that era. It's true, his father might have, would have likely murdered his only son over the shame of being gay. That wife beating drunken veteran would have denied New York it's hottest young designer. Didn't you know that? Oh-no, yeah, no, Mr. Sheldon Downs Jr. is very influential, he's a star, hot property. He's rich, quite wealthy.

THOMAS: Everybody loves Sheldon, Sissy.

BECKY & REBBIE: It's true, everybody loves Sheldon.

MARCUS: I don't.

RUTH: You don't love anything... but I know what you mean, that Sheldon makes me uncomfortable. Is there more of that italian champaign?

REBBIE: Prosecco.

SISSY: ...more uncomfortable.

BECKY: what were you and Sheldon talking about Sophia?

SISSY: Crystal methamphetamine and White Supremacists, We're like sisters. Hey, We're like sisters too Becky, cool. I can't believe you have sex with my brother!

SAM: (*winking*) Oh dear, I was afraid of this Ruth, you should have been warned about Sheldon's corrupting influence, his brand of hypnotic double talk is particularly effective on nubile young women. Like your daughter.

REBBIE: Relax Ruth, my darling man child is just yanking your chain. Sheldon is just being Sheldon.

SHELDON: *(Blasts in, popping cork)* Yeah, I get it. I'm DAUNTING.

REBBIE: Don't let him rattle you Ruth. Everything Sheldon is too too interesting.

BECKY: Every Sheldon story, his life. Is too interesting, it is threatening. Sometimes I'd like to shoot him myself.

RUTH: It's admirable how much he's achieved.

SHELDON: Wowoo, my ears are burning. *(he fills glasses)*

REBBIE: Establishment types, conservatives find gay New Yorkers too challenging.

SAM: Yeah, that's me love, Mr. Conservative- I know what you mean though Marcus, and it's not just a fag thing, There's plenty of queers who hate Sheldon, it's his despicable power.

MARCUS: Amorality. Outrageousness. Friviouslesness.

SHELDON: If I might interject, as if I were right here in the room with you, I AM powerful, I make art that's worth a lot of money, I do what I want...

SISSY: He says what he thinks.

REBBIE: He doesn't care about other people's feelings.

BECKY: No, not exactly, he doesn't care about anybodys bad feelings.

SHELDON: HELLO! I'm right here, at least I have manners, but yes, I calls 'em as I sees 'em. Another's anger? Their rancor, madness, shame, it's not me. Can not. It's on them, You should understand this Sam the man, the original California beach boy gone to pot, it's a very buddhist principle.

SAM: The little fairy's got a mean streak.

RUTH: No kidding, like that comment about my nose, you are insensitive Sheldon.

MARCUS: What comment.

BECKY: Well it's true Ruth, women with big noses shouldn't wear bangs, it's an unflattering hairstyle. For the profile. A strong profile, a, um.

MARCUS: Becky, I see why my son Tom would pick such a girl as you, you are very beautiful, such a pretty young figure, that fuzzy sweater is just, wow...   and very intelligent but if you keep saying stupid things like that to your future mother-in-law you are going to make all of our lives difficult. Sheldon is rude, you're rude Sheldon, It is atrociously bad mannered to say such an obvious thing to my wife at our childrens' engagement party.

REBBIE: Insensitive.

SHELDON: (*sing-song*) INACCURATE! I'm the most sensitive being you've ever met. And humble, but yes Professor, I am atrociously bad mannered. Tee-hee.

SAM: I think it's cool, I like a shit disturber.

SISSY: Me too.

REBBIE: Yeah right, not when he calls you "Fat Bastard", I thought you were gonna punch him.

SAM: *(laughing, putting Sheldon in an uncomfortable locker room head lock)* HAW HA I could've poisoned you, ya little cocksucker.

EVERYBODY: ...daddy!.. Woah SAM... Samuel... Mr. Ford...

SAM: Aw, C'mon, What? Really, Cocksucker?

EVERYBODY: Sam Ford, really, Daddy/ woah

SHELDON: (escaping headlock, fixing hair, *pause*) Butt Fucker?.. Barking silence.

MARCUS: ...Yes, well, um Mr. Downs, in our family we use the term Anal Sex Enthusiast.

SHELDON: Oh yes, Im the rude one.

Later at the same party after further drinking

RUTH: You just interrupted me, they don't want to hear about your boat, your boat that won't float. Sheldon? you don't care about boats. He's been building that stupid boat for years. Let's hear Thommy play his violin again.

THOMAS: *(replacing his mother's empty martini glass with a glass of water)* No Mom, I already played, I've put it away.

REBBIE: That was Mahler? It was beautiful Tom.

THOMAS: Thank you Rebbie, it's Stravinski.

RUTH: Play us another tune on the fiddle.

MARCUS: For Christ Sake Ruth, it's the viola, your son plays the viola, you're embarrassing yourself.

RUTH: I wasn't embarrassing myshelf, It's my self, I was doing a, you know, a conscice psychological connecting the dots about what he said she said, I was... comparing it to the age of anxiety, you know, by the Austrian, Damnit Marcush... Vwallah... Viola- I know Thom plays the Viola, he's done it again. Bully.

SAM: Yes yes Ruth, but Sheldon needs no defending, that's the whole raison d'etre of outrage, it's phony, it's a fake-o, it's not rage, it's false outrage...

SISSY: (*runs in holding a red plastic solo cup doing a lap of the room trailing a paper party decoration streamer*) Pink Tarantula!! (*She exits and is ignored like a 7 year old would be*)

SHELDON: I'm all for clarification.

SAM: Condescending little snob ass fag. Just because it occurs to you, because you are insightful or bright or lucid, doesn't mean you should- or does mean rather, you shouldn't comment on it. She's entitled to any idiotic point of view with no merit what-so-ever which she may have kicking around in her, her , head-

BECKY: -Daddy.

SAM: you talk too much Sheldon.

SHELDON: Rather. Indeed. As do we all, because you love me Samuel, I shall refrain from further cynical witticisms.

SAM: I hate you.

SHELDON: Same thing.

RUTH: Psychopaths.

SAM: *(toasts a glass clink with Sheldon)* Yeah Sheldon, put a cock in it- a cork, a cork!

SHELDON: I'm gonna make sure Sissy keeps off the roof, more prosecco?

RUTH: Shes fine.

THOMAS: That was the last bottle Shell.

MARCUS: I've got a case of gin in the Subaru, *(He tosses Thomas his keys)*

THOMAS: Great.

later after more drinking

MARCUS: Oh really.

SAM: Yes Really Marcus, I said it, I meant it.

MARCUS: What a youthful turn of phrase, but Sam, how could that be.

SAM: Oh come on, fuck that didactical, accusatory horse shit- "How could that be." It's a Fact. Samuel Leghorn Clemens was a total bigot. The facts will bear me out on this, experts agree.

MARCUS: Fallacious appeal to authority. It's Langhorn.

SAM: Everybody was a bigot, everyone Is a bigot.

MARCUS: My point exactly, therefore no one was. Is. (*they stop to consider this last statement*) So yeah... I guess we agree. You know it's Langhorn.

SAM: Of course I know. I know everything about all of Twain's river writing, I'm an expert. I'm The expert.

MARCUS: Oh. I see. So you wanna do it, are we on? (*he extends hand to shake on a bet*)

SAM: What? Really?

MARCUS: Yes really, I said it I meant it. So yes, it's your challenge, or are you all hat?-   ? You won't though.

SAM: Says you.

MARCUS: Prove me wrong. It's a game of chicken, are you seeing this Hon? Oh god, she's asleep? Sissy make sure your mother isn't going to choke on her own vomit. You see this son, your father in law to be is made of sand.

THOMAS: Wait, what now, what's at stake?

MARCUS: Poop Deck Pappy over here said I wouldn't last a day on the river, I gave him multiple chances to save face, thinks he knows more than any old book learned academic American Literature Ph.D. and tested blue water mariner.

THOMAS: Sam, I have never in 26 years heard my father brag, what have you done to my father? Oh shit dad, are you really falling for this, Are you actually trying to out macho Mr. Ford.

SAM: Tom my boy, call me POP. I'm afraid your father ain't as smart as he thinks.

MARCUS: Fish or cut bait, I did my dissertation on Twain and have been on 4 offshore sailing passages.

THOMAS: Dad, Key west to Key largo isn't exactly a grand banks cod fisherman.

MARCUS: Nope he'll never do it, he won't even take the bet, I know the type. (*Sam spits into his palm takes Marcus's hand and won't let go, dueling cowboys*)

SISSY: Why don't you guys arm wrestle.

SHELDON: (*entering with Rebbie, smoking pot which they share with Sissy*) Oh boy, recognize this one Rebbie? Who's demanding satisfaction from whom? SUH! (*Becky follows, declines pot*)

REBBIE: (*handing Sissy the joint*) Alright now I want you to observe Lil'Bit, this is a teaching moment, because you see, they are old sorry men, still boys, grey haired boys, afraid of the grave, old grave dying men... and actual patriarchy-

SHELDON: - Oh wow, such big strong men with such big strong brains, it makes my blood boil-

REBBIE: -and as father figures-*(still sharing pot with Sissy)*

BECKY: - figuratively and literally-

THOMAS:-literaturely.

REBBIE: AND as father figures, that can not possibly make your blood boil; can they Sissy?

SISSY: Eeeew.

REBBIE: Good. The inappropriate boyish behavior of these men, being indicative of the core of all men-

SHELDON: Sexist.

REBBIE: Most men, these overgrown boys and their games, this has got to be a contributing cause of the sophomore lesbian syndrome, ah darling I envy you.

SISSY & SHELDON: Eeeeww.

BECKY: What's the wager.

THOMAS: Nothing. Virility?

MARCUS: Granted, it's a pissing contest, we're seeing who balks first in this protracted game of chicken.

SAM: You will.

MARCUS: No, it'll be you.

BECKY: Stop. What? What is the challenge, what exactly is at stake in this particular gay chicken fight?

SISSY: These two are gonna get on a Robinson Crusoe Boat.

THOMAS: No Sissy, a Huckleberry Finn Raft.

REBBIE: Whatever, no they aren't, they're going to collude to excuse each other from this hoax.

SHELDON: And then accuse each other of being pussies. It's outrageous. It's scandalous!

BECKY: Yes, fine, of course, I know, but what is it exactly that they're not going to do.

MARCUS & SAM: We are!

SHELDON: Wooowo, pinky shake.

BECKY: What? What is it?

SAM: Ivory tower over here started it Sweetpea, he claims to KNOW Mark Twain's intent...

MARCUS: ...and Bryan Wilson over here thinks that a raft trip down an American river would prove who's who and what's what.

BECKY & REBBIE: Well that's stupid. (*they pinky shake with Sheldon and Sissy reacting*)

SAM: No, what I said was, let me clarify, OK? Thus: Two men, mature thinking visceral men, pilot a rafting adventure down the?-

MARCUS: Potomac.

SAM: - steer a rustic vessel down the mighty Potomac, past the capitol of the free world, down the brackish Potomac all the way to the mouth of the great Chesapeake, crossing this great nation's largest estuary from Maryland- the old line state to the Old Dominion of olde Virginny.

MARCUS: Ah gracious! Rest-stop diner place-mat clap trap...

SAM: OK, OK quitter, we're on, or you are a, quitter. "Sir I challenge you to a duel!"

MARCUS: I accept.

REBBIE: Jesus Christ in a fucking garter belt.

BECKY, SISSY, THOMAS: Oh god / amazing, oh shit, is this really happening?...

SHELDON: Soooo gay.

SISSY: I know right.

Act II

Becky and Thomas in wedding day finery are flanked by Sheldon and Sissy as best man and maid of honor with the in law moms and dads paired with each others spouse book ending a big semi circular wedding photo tableau. The party shifts positions as a photographer might pose them in pairs, trios and groups. The lines are delivered both realistically as between photo banter but also express thoughts unspoken. The fathers are decked out in the costumes of their raft trip. Occasional frozen shutter clicks and flashes punctuate. This choreographed section builds and welcomes absurdly creative interpretation but is not however a song and dance production number. Perhaps it's a sad slow waltz. Audibly there are glasses clinking and breaking, chairs dragging, silverware on china, bass drop whoops and claps of disco dance band feedback, splashing water, clomping marching footfalls, seagulls and car horns, squealing tires, a siren and church organ music. The crack of a broken stiletto heel. This scene won't direct itself. Mix it up.

BECKY: It was really nice, it was nice, I'm not really one for that "Greatest day of my life" business, but it was fine.

THOMAS: It was nice... What, more? It was really nice. Um. The weather cooperated, at least until we left for the airport. Becky looked fantastic, well you saw the pictures, I was kind of uncomfortable in the monkey suit. Yeah, and Mom crying. That was awkward.

RUTH: *(sobbing hard)* Oh Tommy, so handsome, my beautiful Tommy-Tom, my beautiful boy, whaaa, shlobber, snorf-

THOMAS: Mom over drank.

SHELDON: The bitch was De-runk.

RUTH: Tom a llama ding dong korful -snorf -taaaaeeeoooOOWWWoomee boy..

REBBIE: Yikes, somebody's meds need a little tweeking.

SISSY: What happened was mom got into my thermos of (*air quotes*) "Calming Tea", that I brought, to party with Sheldon and Jon Louis at the reception. I feel bad, but it was pretty amusing. Until it was horrendous. Mushrooms last a long time.

SHELDON: That house of rubber chicken entree couldn't have cost too much, I hope the balance went to the dowery. Ooww Thomas cut a very dashing figure in the Armani. Let's see- fashion police! Rebbie was in her usual split back wedding mumu with come fuck me pumps, Jon Louis I dressed myself so no problem there, Little Sissy had on some apocalyptic mad max emu thing the kids like, she pulled it off, the torpedo brasier pretty much steers that boat. I of course rocked the red. The bride, I love her, I've loved her since summer camp, yes I was a counselor- Not a thing wrong with a single hair, not a thread or lash out of place, poise, classically beautiful, neither fat nor lean, regal and pure. But in the final analysis, meh. Like a million others. Mission accomplished. (*shrug*) The Dads with their safari outfits, Jimmy Buffett meets Marlin Perkins... and then there was the Mother of the groom. Ruth. Dear lord Ruth. Frump, hempen homespun frump. And full of mead, or ergot, - piss and vinegar? Absinthe? Paint thinner?

RUTH: A toast to the beauty of our children, may the road come up to meet their journey of a thousand cuts starting with the next day of the rest of our liveliness. Humana humana. Squiggly lines. Hot hard thump beat of the disco fever dance. The dance of paleo-vegan flesh eaters. HUNGER. Hunger. hung. gun. gough. This is wrong. I'm going to. to. too. toot tootsie gomba. goooooomba. gooooooo-

SAM: Can you believe it? This whole thing for 6000, I know a caterer. See if ya' give like a quarter of the posted deposit like 3 months out, right, and then you threaten to dump, well, the hotels will always sweeten the deal with a load of bumps to keep the party, I know the beverage manager. I know this game. It's my milieu, pardon my french. This is a great place for hookers, you wanna get a hooker, Marko? You want a hooker don't you? I got us a gentlemen's' room, it's a suite, a suite-ette, great deal, super swank, but there's some painting and sheetrock decorators shit stored there in the wine closet. it's really cool, it's round the back stairs of the far wing, second floor, no shit. Jacuzzi. Here, take the key card, no other dudes unless they bring extra broads, just you and me. I got cigars, I got gin, a little toot. They got these great hookers around the corner, Filipinas, I know the concierge. It ain't cheap but it's nice right, I have one daughter, it ain't cheap, quality ain't cheap.

SHELDON: Oh it's cheap.

SISSY: Yeah it is.

MARCUS: Yes it is cheap. Wholly adequately cheap, it's generously cheap. You thank the man Thomas, I'm sure he's doing his level best. Economy. A tradition of economy. There is no creativity without waste, but, well... Ahhh my son. The tradition of the father of the bride footing the wedding bill, it's a, an. Um, a tradition, it is good, it's good of him, Sam the man. I'm sure you've thanked him, you don't hafta thank him. I've thanked him. Thank god that part's over.

THOMAS: I think it's actually Rebbie's family money.

MARCUS: No matter, it still speaks to the man's mettle, marrying up like that, punching above his weight as it were, eh what, smell what I'm cooking old sport... So um, in keeping alive the traditional spirit, ritual, keep the old expectations alive, life! A man, don't you know old sport, on the occasion of his only son's nuptials has responsibilities on his son's nuptials. Thomas, a little advice from father to son on his wedding night.

THOMAS: I'm afraid where this is going dad.

MARCUS: Your wife will never look as good as she does right now, tonight. Her glowing radiance, her smell, the brief singularly erotic high point awaits you, before the duties and responsibilities of earning and children and automobile insurance and first and second and third mortgages force one to abandon any artistic aspirations and you are cursed with the crushing yoke of debt and the dreamless hair shirt of reality. Leaving your life as a proud buck you have to seize the antlers of your doe. A bull moose in musk, we are but animals after all my first born, my only son. So. Unwrap that wedding dress gift package with verve and gusto my son, tonight she is yours. You will pay with your soul. I'm sorry I failed you, my son and moon and stars. I'm sorry I've failed myself.

THOMAS: ...Seize the antlers. All right Da, I hear you.

REBBIE: Sophie, Sheldon's heard this and Becky's ignored this to try and hurt me, but I want you to know, there is no justification in the world for getting married. Even if you find the perfect soul mate and want to publicly state a commitment and feel you need to have a celebration to suck up all the attention to validate the dark hole of fear at your center with a silly pseudo religious bacchanal, there is still no reason what-so-ever to ever get married.

BECKY: Taxes Mom, it's financially wise to file jointly.

THOMAS: And for the kids.

REBBIE: I'm talking to Sophia here. Oh and horseshit, you don't have to pay taxes, it is incumbent upon a principled citizenry to Not pay taxes. Children crave choices, they seek freedom, they don't need to have their parents model enslavement. Sam and I never tied any legal knot and we're the better for it.

SISSY: Mr. Ford just put his hand on my ass, so did Rebbie, I kissed a waiter.

BECKY: No Mom, you need to pay taxes, in the real world you

have to pay your taxes, I'm not having children.

THOMAS: What?

BECKY: Ever.

SAM: Rebbie won't sleep with me any more.

MARCUS: Sorry to hear that.

SAM: We used to do a lot of role playing. In the bedroom.

MARCUS: Sorry to have learned that.

SAM: Master slave stuff, a lotta bondage, ass stuff, everything.

MARCUS: OK, keep it to yourself.

RUTH: Your father hasn't touched me in years.

SISSY: Ma, you're over excited, would you like to sit down, would you like me to duct tape you to a chair?

SHELDON: -and lock you in a closet?

SISSY: -with a rabid rottweiler, and burn down the building with you in it?

RUTH: The throbbing pulsing jungle drumble of bodies co-mangled, thrumping the incarnadine jasmine jump boogaloo, my hands, my hands, my hips, the loins, olfactory compulsion of loins, the lion roaring of breasts and that Gigantic frozen phallus, glaumana glaumana glaumana glaumana.

MARCUS: Oh my god, that dance floor-

SHELDON: That poor ice sculpture.

SAM: CHEESE!

REBBIE: Poor Marcus, no wonder he's wound so tight, I could clean his clock.

SAM: Poor Ruth, her head looks like a watermelon.

SISSY: Poor poor pitiful me, I could slit my wrists.

MARCUS: And so that very night-

THOMAS: As I and my passionless bride-

BECKY: -slept in a hotel room overlooking a third world sea-

SISSY: and I baby sat my dosed and confused mother in the emergency waiting room-

SHELDON: And Jon Louis and I snorted coke and spied through the bushes at-

REBBIE: Me and that sturdy young waiter in the hot tub-

SAM: Marcus and I went down to the river under moonbeams and mosquitoes-

MARCUS: With smoking cigars and bottles of gin-

SAM: Pushing off from the shore, past loons and the thrushes-

MARCUS: Beyond eddies and wakes-

SAM: On out to the middle, the shore sliding up stream, so still in our movement-

MARCUS: -we mumbled and staggered. We sang.

SAM: We pissed in the river then slept.

END SCENE

ACT III

A long dumb show, dawn to sunset where the two fathers travel in boredom, Safari wedding outfits soiled and tattered, punting, washing dishes, fishing, drinking, smoking, reading, lazing about, the sky is a show of clouds, yellow dawn, blues & whites ending with orange and purple sunset, Contemporary stagecraft audio / visual smorgasbord. The raft drifts and bobs and spins traveling through the playing area, time, space and the cosmos.

Time passing segue stagecraft flapdoodle scene to:

Daylight on the raft: *(in grey fog the scene opens mid assault as the madman from the ramshackle houseboat reels about the deck of their Huckleberry Finn holiday raft. He is brandishing a loaded shotgun. He is graceful and ranting, wild eyed under fright wig and snaggle toothed grimace. Jackie Gleason on speed.)*

THE SURVIVALIST: (*Actor who plays Sheldon transformed*) No? Nothing? No crafty rejoinder? ...one big fuckin' dissapointment after another, no gifts from the successful, the privileged, you dumbassed lucky worthless motherfuckers. What're you? Slumming it? Blog-hiccough-Bloggers! The Fortunate have earned all the resentment the ignored can muster. Just 'cause it happened to you don't mean it's interesting, keep it to yourselfish assed selves why don't chu?! The Anger is all there is. The haves owe the have nots EVERYTHING. Motherfuckers might as well die, or steal, there is no meritocracy. Crime or suicide... or substance abuse, or a good old fashioned American Hermitage, or all of the above, give me some of your Gin, shit Gin, drink of imperialists. Give me liberty. Beefeater fuckin gin. Martini Gin, let me swill your toffee bottomed high class low class gin.. Pajama bloggers, assholes! ... Where's the break?! HUH!?! Where is would you please tell me the fucking advantage. None! No chance to progress. Fuck-it. Fuck-it. Fuck-it. No foundation all the way down the line 'liddle monkey faces, don't be a fool, buy me a 'trink, gimmie the fuckin' plastic bottle of Gin or I'll shoot you both dead with this sawed off shotgun! (*they do*) Now go. SCRAM, you heard me, BLOW! I'm ready to die but I'd rather kill. Kill the Brain! Bite the worm, Die yuppie scum. Ivory tower assholes. Federalists. Zombies. Fuck off and die. I need to plot my revenge right now. Alone. All alone and drunk all along the lazy river of doom, you are lucky again, you are lucky this time, again. (*He fires the shotgun into their cooking tripod blasting the ashes and dutch oven and scattering noisy pie tins and cans and silverware*) I'm taking your inflatable, it's aesthetically incongruent. *(He deftly casts off and skips onto the deck of his own craft.)* Again and again time after time you lucky privileged parasites survive, SOMEHOW. (*pause, from a distance as the river opens up between them*) GO TO HELL. BACK TO

FUCKIN' HELL, MOTHERFUCKERS. Blog my dick." (*He throws a busted lawnchair from a distance at the traumatized rusticating mariners alone again on their violated raft*) Get off my river. May all your sons be Jesuits. Bitches... Blech! Gin!

Scene segues, time, shadow and light, sounds of birdsong and banjos, babbling tributaries, off key pianos and women's voices harmonizing a little tune, smooth dissonance without resolve.

The two at opposite corners of the raft lost in their own thoughts, moon gazing and star watching as the planetarium milky way sky revolves and rotates its early summer circuit, the raft at center stage describes a slow turn or two in the opposite direction as the spin of the heavens.

Scene segues darker, darker still, candles.

(Sam and Marcus on the raft, dark, fire in a galvanized bucket atop a cinderblock, drinking gin, smoking cigars and weed and talking over deep and hitherto unexpressed thoughts about art, love and desire.)

MARCUS: (*After a perplexed pause*)... That's the purpose of Love? I thought we established there is no purpose of love, that it doesn't exist.

SAM: No, Writing, not Love. We haven't established anything, great writers, the poets have established there is no love. Or, writing On love is Not love, well love transcends language, even though there is an language of love.

MARCUS: An language? is that even english- I thought you just said, hey don't drink all my gin, didn't you just say the one true purpose of love is...

SAM: NO NO NO NO NO NO NO , No the one true purpose of writin'-

MARCUS: -Creative writing.

SAM: Yes of course Creative writing, what else, whaddya think, technical writing, legal writing... What? What other kinds writin' is there?

MARCUS: Um...Medical... wri-...ting?

SAM: Sure, Journalism, all that secondary text horse shit. Comparative Lit, comprehensive under-grad academic dreck.

MARCUS: Excuse me... That happens to be my profession, that's where I've made my living and raised my family with, on, I'll have you know, thank you very much... Tavern keeper.

SAM: It's a living, you just rattled off about a hundred unnecessary words, I'll have you know excuse me, thank you very much, I'll have you know Bartending, capitol B, happened to have raised my family. It's the purpose of an educated man to take a difficult concept and transform it into a comprehensible idea, you've just done the opposite, again, as does all your ilk... Civil servant.

MARCUS: Lot of purpose to this conversation. ILK? I don't have an ilk.

SAM: Oh don't you, I think you're pretty ilky?

MARCUS: No I don't. I'm singularly very unique.

SAM; Whaa, one is Singularly, or very, or unique, don't you know...Ghaaa! The fraud committed on our kids by these universities, the theft of these astronomical tuitions, I'm besides m, my... (Sputters outraged...)

MARCUS; SAM... SAMUEL...Of course, you don't really think I'm...

SAM; Very unique! Unique is not Very! my God. . . The crushing yoke of debt these student loans burden our kids, our entire society with.....

MARCUS: Sam, shut up. I teach the elements of style for fucks sake, you humorless blowhard.

SAM: ...Oh, ...oh shit, what a fool, touche'. Me humorless, you bastard, that's just mean Marcus, I'm not humorless..

MARCUS: I know that. You're not... Humor less. You are Humorful.

SAM: Humorous... oh shit, you got me again. Fuckeree. Fuck.

MARCUS: Look Sam it's OK, disparage my profession, I'm fed up with it, you're mostly right, I Agree with you, but I'm not the didactic smug bastard on this little boat, alright so get off my tits.

SAM: *(pause)*... Raft, not boat. Professor.

MARCUS: So you wanna be Mr. Howell or Gilligan or what.

SAM: Ginger, I wanna be Ginger and I want you to be Mary Ann and I wanna tie your little farm girl bikini bottoms around your

48

pony tailed neck in a lezbo shipwreck scurvyied sex halicunation.

MARCUS: Oh-god, you are fuckin' funny Sammy. You're a poet.

SAM: Which is the point I'm making, Writing's one true purpose, creative writings raison d'etre 'S poetry. That is why we should have been taught by our parents to read. Poetry, or speak it...

MARCUS: Poetry shmoetery, honestly? I don't like to read poetry, truth be told, it leaves me flat, can't even read those shortys in the New Yorker.

SAM.: Not to read (*Reed)*, to be read (*Red)*, aloud, in public. Poetry must be read aloud. Performed.

MARCUS: Oh god No. Stop! You don't mean, you can't possibly mean... Slam?!

SAM: Oh Shit Mark, do I look like a dreadlocked 23 year old? No not Slam, no, not Slam. No. Just to be read aloud. Performed. Not even necessarily for an audience.

MARCUS: Performed, but not for an audience? Excuse me but what is your definition of the word perform?

SAM: You, know? To perform, to carry out, to do, to execute.

MARCUS: OK. I'm with you there, let's execute all poems, and Poets too while you're at it. Take care of the job once and for always.

SAM: Well I rest my fucking case, here you are an English teacher, administrator whatever, with a total disregard for language, entrusted with, what, I dunno, extracting as much of their parents money as you can from these doe eyed brats, you are a cog Marcus is all, you're just a cog in the industrial education complex not giving 'em anything, not a damn thing, just taking.

MARCUS

Not true, I'm giving 'em the business, teaching 'em a lesson, it's the humanities Sam, not accounting, there not coming out of an American liberal arts college with an H.V.A.C. certification, a boiler operator level 3 licence. I'm giving an emerging adult a taste of what is inevitably to follow. You appreciate the Arts, and letters? Fine. Good. But lookie here friend, the pinnacle of those worlds, the opera houses, and museums, and universities, broadway, hollywood, each example more fraudulent than the last, that calling is peopled with nothing but charlatans and wannabes and inebriates holding the keys of locked doors against armies of talented dancers and poets and writers and musicians and philosophers, the very worst thing for art is successful artists. And what if I did teach the hard sciences, then what, read the paper if you can find one, not the sunday metro, not between the lines, read the damn headlines. There are no jobs in America, take your kitty litter diploma back to mom's basement and sleep on the couch, we're all doomed and there is no point in trying because it's hopeless. My deadened soul ineffectually parroting literary curriculum to disinterested undergrads is the least of the larceny committed by the university, look at the food and lodging markup, look at the football program, look at the law schools and numbskull business schools, what are they providing, how are their billable hours helping this planet? I'm ready to slit my own throat Sam. Have you seen my Wife, have you ever seen an uglier woman?! Why else would I take this inane raft trip, I'm here to end this fearful slumber, I'm here to die. You guzzled all the gin, you fat fuck! How could you Sam, I cannot live another sober moment, you've killed me with that last swallow. Put in, I need to find a liquor store.

SAM: Relax, we've got a box of wine.

MARCUS: I'm not drinking wine from a box, screw it, I'll swim to shore. *(Marcus dives off of raft)*

SAM: Oh shit, you drunken idiot, Marcus....Marcus..... Marcus.....Marcus.....   Marcus, Marcus....Marcus.....

Marcus.....Marcus.....Marcus....Marcus.....
END SCENE

ACT IV At the inquisition.

(*Indoors at a fancy room, dark wood paneling, reflective polished wood*)

SAM: Yeah, no, yeah right, I said to him I said straight out: Touche' my friend; not my friend, whatever the hell you are, were, family? father-in-brother-in-law? Our children were married you see, and so what we did was, was we hatched this silly scheme in inebriated get togethers, you know, at functions, at the wedding and the engagement party, at picnics and what not. If Marcus had ever of walked into my pub, The Poetic Patriot, I'd never have given him a second look, I'd of written him off as a tourist, a square, and I'm sure the same for the other different, he thinks I'm a blowhard because, well I am. But it was the Huckleberry Finn thing. Wouldnt'a given him the time a day, but for Mark Twain. See?.. Long ago I'd decided that was to be my subject of expertise, the subject I could hold forth on at the Pub. On poets night and among the pickled regulars. I thought it made sense. About any topical news story or sociological current event, psychology or americana discussion, I'd be able to have a Twain quote or aphorism at the ready and could preface my blinding insightful analogies with the intro: "It's like when Injun Joe is trapped in the cave" or other cryptic half thoughts such as "Pap Finn's bloated corpse in the flooded house", it was easy, I didn't even need to read the books, there's so much secondary Twain scribbling. And after the internet- Forget about it. I needed to be an authority on something as impresario of my west coast college town irish bar. It'd never of flown on the east coast, my signature subject would'a needed some kinda Hibernian flavor ya' understand. I actually hate the Irish, their sentimental poets, the pipes, those unintelligible shanty drunken maudlin ballads, and all that didley- dydely dung heap music. Fuck Joyce, nobody understands that shit. Kerouac is more readable. My celtic surname is my stepfathers, and it was his stepfathers. I'm actually a Heinz 57 mutt, mostly mexican. I cannot speak or understand spanish, even having heard it my entire life, somewhere obviously deciding we pick our heritage more than it picks us. I dropped out of U.C. Santa Cruz for christ sake. The fighting banana slugs. Nothing, you see, nothing is authentic. If you claim to be a fraud and a liar you are neither. Anywho I was sure I had Marcus trumped on the Mark Twain lore, I thought I knew his type. But as it turned out Marcus had me in spades, I underestimated his depth. I assumed he, like all professionals, like you own self yourself your Hone-er, I just figured Sam was either the duke or the King not Huck or Clemens, but in the end he was Tom Sawyer. I suppose. That's what I say about him anyhow, I can't be proved wrong and that has always been as right as I've ever been about anything.

THE INQUISITOR: (*played by Sheldon in a barristers wig & robe, not as fully transformed as the Survivalist but stuffier than the Sheldon we met in the first and second acts,. He's seated in a throne like chair, his feet shod in resplendent sequined pumps rest atop a stack of law books and bibles.*) Fascinating. Mr.Ford, do you know why you are here?

SAM: Um, yeah! Do you know why I'm here?

THE INQUISITOR: We seek clarity.

SAM: Verily. So what's the implication, should I not be so thorough?

THE INQUISITOR: We didn't invite you here to make a toast.

SAM: You said it, I was Invited, not subpoenaed, you are trying to come to agreement over his estate, do the the right thing with his things and settle his debts and stuff, correct?

THE INQUISITOR: Surprisingly succinct.

SAM: He owes me nothing, I bear no claim to any of his assets, and I sure as shit don't owe him a God damn thing. You actually have

55

no juice to subpoena if I am not mistaken, and even iffin you did I'd lie to you... Bitch.

THE INQUISITOR: *(pause)* How very colorful. You're here to aid in answering the question of what happened to Dr.Sheppard on the night in question, and let me remind you...

SAM: I'm here as a favor. I'm attempting to make clear my complete disregard for all institutions, except maybe the Bay View Boat Club, but this body, the insurance companies, the backward state government Marco's university and employer represents, all lawyers, judges, professionals of any kind. You guys, your ilk can kiss my fat Irish Mexican ass.

THE INQUISITOR: Sir, you must comply...

SAM: Don't sir me, Why must I comply? How am I compelled to comply? If you would like to establish he died so the vultures can pick his non existent corpse well, I'm not sure how I feel about all that.

THE INQUISITOR: Oh for Pete's sake. How about for the sake of brevity then.

SAM: I'll explain it how I see fit, you want to save time, then stop interrupting then.

THE INQUISITOR: Ugh... Well?

SAM: Next question.

THE INQUISITOR: (*pause*) May I ask you to describe the moments leading up to the point at which Prof- Marcus Shepard dove off the raft into the water?

SAM: Yes you may ask.

THE INQUISITOR: Oh Christ... Well, What happened?

SAM: How the hell should I know, we were drunk for a week, over 300 miles of river, it all looked the same, one day was like another. You ever even been camping pussy?

THE INQUISITOR: OUT! Get this man the fuck out of here, go, get him out of here. (*Sam man handles and bum's rushes himself off the dock*)... You know he's right, it doesn't matter if Mr. Shepard is dead or not, if that idiot killed him, or not, it's not my concern if he drowned in a gin soaked mistake. If he ascended to heaven in a one man rapture. Spaceman abduction, I DON'T CARE. He is delinquent in all his affairs and has lost all control over what happens to his estate. It hardly matters if he is even dead. But now, in a free society there are certain rules, unfortunately at this hearing all concerned parties get a... hearing. Um lets see, (*checks stack of papers*) alright, it's the wife's turn now I suppose, um, do you wish to speak Mrs. Sheppard?

RUTH: I've retaken my maiden name. Ms. Glick if you please.

THE INQUISITOR: Really? You think that's better? Actually, Mizz Glick, until this inquiry is over you are technically still Mrs. Sheppard- but why split hairs, prithee continue miss... Bla bla, 12th of May, year of our lord etcetera, testimony of Mrs. Ruth Sheppard, A.K.A. Miss Ruth Awkberg Glick. -but what's in a name. The required 12 months have passed since the first citation when the waiting period writ was granted...

RUTH: It's been a year? It's been longer than that, It's been years, he may have left us physically a year ago, more, but the estates legal incubation period started 14 months ago. He's been gone, or dead to me, since I became a burden to him, since my youngest, my only daughter was born, since I was pregnant with Sophia. I will not call her Lil'Bit. I won't call her Sissy either. I wouldn't call her Spinach or Trash or any of her other nicknames. Not even Sophie. Her name is Sophia, I named her that after my aunt. My Aunt who was insane. My daughter is also emotionally disabled. I never should have had children. Sophia loved her father and blames me for everything, but he left me 20 years ago. With the money from the settlement I am going away, I'm moving overseas, I won't say where, it doesn't matter, paradise is not a place. Many places are not hell though, I am leaving hell. I'm stuck here now on earth wherever that is until I die. And then? Then I will be dead. At least I'll have money enough to eat.

My son is without need of me, with his whore. His offspring is entitled to a portion of this estate I gather. c'est la vie.

Divorce or separation or sickness or other crisis or death. That's the probably list I've lived with for years, and I can't tell if it's what makes me hopeless or if my hopelessness made this list. Wealth, ease, leisure, travel, adventure, intimacy, companionship, success, meaning and reward just don't seem likely, haven't since before I was married, it's hard to have any fun without a dirty joke, a vice or a mistake. If you want to know what you want, look at what you've got. I don't deserve this life I'm faced with, I am not being punished, I was just gypped. You have the letter I believe sir.

THE INQUISITOR: Wow. What? Oh yeah. I have it here Miss Glick. You should like to hear it now I gather.

RUTH: Ha, of course not, but isn't it required?

THE INQUISITOR: -UM, er yes, that is the procedure, now is the time if you have said your peace.

RUTH: Sure, whatever, get it done... What do you want? An invitation?

THE INQUISITOR: I've never encountered such a rude bunch as this, (*He opens a sealed envelope*) This communication was found in the backyard half finished sailboat used as an office by Professor Shepard. It was reportedly found by his only daughter, Sophia Sheppard a week after his disappearance was reported.

SISSY: I go by the name Spinach now.

THE INQUISITOR: I'm not going to call you Spinach young lady.

SISSY: I found it with my brother, it was sticking out of the old Royal Safari manual typewriter in the Shelby, that was his boat, it was more than half finished, it was beautiful, it was almost done, he was gonna sail it to Ireland, My Ex-Mother had no right to have it destroyed, it was my dowery, My-Ex mother is a bitch, I'm gonna burn down her house, I'm gonna turn her body into soap. You should see what he wrote on his e-mails and instant messages, I know his password, he had girlfriends Mother, more than one, a few, he hated you. You cunt.

THE INQUISITOR: Yes, as you've stated in your testimony earlier, twice. And in your letters and filings and at the deposition, we are all aware of your, ideas. Please stop talking.

SISSY: Fuck your own mother, chimpanzee.

THE INQUISITOR: See what I'm up against, savages, each one less courteous than the last, shut her up or throw her out. I read now from the letter as I am compelled to do:

MARCUS: (i*n drowned ghost of Christmas past ghoul trappings*) Not all that much has changed since we were young, maintaining responsible passionless sloppy housekeeping. I genuinely used to admire Ruth's looks and poise and traits and brains, she gave the world 2 fine children who are special people and I'm proud to share their last name, but it pisses me off that she only permits me to stay, that she doesn't admire me, that I never really set her on fire. To be tolerated is so close to being ignored that it can feel the same; a sort of no feeling.
I can give up smoking and drinking again, clearly I can survive without intimacy, frustrations without fireworks is a lot easier the older I grow and fussing and fighting is just awful and pointless and stupid, but I don't know if I want to give up my oldest closest friend: Unhappiness. My sadness or disappointment or anger or

depression or whatever description is given to these not so rare moods is as much a part of me as my wit and impulsiveness and voice and gait. My job means nothing, has always meant nothing. I essentially work for a hotel chain. Academia is shit. Academia is shit. My eyes, hair, teeth, waistline are going. I have never felt adequately loved by the half a dozen women who've mattered the most. I have no real friends. Fundamentally philosophically this is outrageous, should be viewed as outrageous, which I define as a condition that warrants rage. One way one can accept the unacceptable is to feel and in my case act unhappy, but I suppose avoiding feelings, or at least practicing not showing them might be a way to eventually no longer feel them. It's unlikely that all feelings would cease, something would sneak in. Maybe even occasional happiness. Of course I'd rather be wasted, I think I'm a failure, and that hurts my feelings. I fail to see the likelihood that things will improve, I lack hope. I remain compelled towards the sex act still, though not with my wife, Ruth the rutabega. The unmarried and divorced barren women from my past are flirted with in my internet correspondences, and a couple of three actual liaisons have staved off outright suicide, but the amount of alcohol required to bed these poor old women leaves the memory of the act clouded, there is very little purchase to the replaying of these exploits, I remember the disheveled hangovers only. Shame. Shame on me. I mean to quit drinking. I have quit. Frequently. Forgive drinking, or don't? It's supposed to be a disease, an ailment. But is it ever really considered a sickness, don't you always harbor some resentment towards the drunk, for being drunk, for drinking the shit, for pouring it down their own stupid throat. Stupidity and selfishness are rarely compassionately forgiven. There is always a grudge. I need help? I need a drink? Leave me alone, or love me. Goodbye cruel world. I sail away to Shelby in the Shelby.

THE INQUISITOR: What's with this Shelby business, Shelby represents what? It is a metaphor? An inside joke? Who's Shelby.

THOMAS: Sir, if I may? I might be able to bring some clarity to this subject.

THE INQUISITOR: Oh god yes, thank you. Yes young man, please, the only island of manners and morals among this whole ill-begotten clan, please speak.

THOMAS: You are obviously unaware that I have recently left my pregnant wife for her own mother.

THE INQUISITOR: Oh god...

THOMAS: Yeah, I get that... Shelby was Dad's joke, his project. He was building a wooden sailboat in the backyard, like other suburban dads might restore a Ford Mustang Shelby race car, something they're never going to finish, something to putter at while they drink beer with the neighbors, except Da drank alone. The good ship Shelby turned into his office, his man-cave. A place to get away from mother to drink gin and work on his writing, supposedly.

MARCUS: True, I did not produce any great volume of literary fiction, but I taught myself the use of the computer, no easy undertaking for a mature humanities scholar of my generation.

THOMAS: It was his rustic writers retreat. Sissy- Sophia hacked into his browser history; He watched a lot of rather pedestrian porn out there and developed clumsy social network liaisons with old girlfriends from his college days. Sissy is fascinated with these women.

MARCUS: They reached out to me. I was going to finish that boat, I was in the home stretch. It needed another 400 hours tops. It was named Shelby after our neighbor's little girl. The O'Briens. They lived next door, they were renters. They had a little baby, I made friends with Shelby over the garden fence right after we moved in. I'd go into the backyard and talk to her. It was weird living in a house for the first time in my life, the suburbs, very freaky, I owned a park, landed fucking gentry- the bank owned it. We are all renters. What? Shelby. She was an old soul. That cracker box was the first house I ever lived in, my first non apartment building dwelling. She was an amazing little girl, they moved back home to Ireland when she was eleven, her parents were British nationals working at the university. I loved Shelby, she was sweet, like custard. She told me to build that sailboat to come and visit her across the Atlantic. I would do anything that little girl asked. Shelby saw an angel, she talked to a fox. She could untie any knot tangled into a piece of string or an extension cord, Shelby could get it undone. She was very smart, graceful. Very Beautiful. Hair red as iodine. I was almost finished with the boat, I was going to launch her and disappear and find Shelby south west of the North Sea. We were going to live on an island and harvest seaweed, keep a lighthouse, shelter otters. We were never going to be as happy as we were talking over the backyard fence when she sat in her purple dress making daisy chains whilst I pretended to fix the lawnmower.

SISSY: I never saw dad use the lawnmower, I didn't think we owned one.

THOMAS: No he never used the lawnmower.

RUTH: He never even started it up.

MARCUS: It wouldn't start, it was broken. I make no apology. I was broken.

RUTH: I never heard him apologize, he was a very honest man. He never shoveled a single scoop of snow either. Marcus had not sawn a board, painted a spar, hammered a rivet on that lousy boat for the last 9 years of our marriage.

SISSY: You talk about him like he's dead!

THE INQUISITOR: Indeed. As should we all. All right, it'll be good to be done with this sordid affair, barring any further testimony, I think we can pronounce the prescribed disbursement decision, as per section 113 point 86 of the...

REBBIE: I believe I may have some insights into this case sir.

THE INQUISITOR: And you are?

BECKY: That woman is my natural born mother, Rebbie Grainger, common law hose bag to Thomas Shepard, my estranged husband and father to my unborn twins, son of Marcus Shepard, the star of our show.

REBBIE: I believe sir that Marcus Sheppard is not in fact...

BECKY: No Mom, you don't get to speak, your input is not allowable, you shall not be recognized.

THE INQUISITOR: Ah, the son in law fucker. Zip it or prepare to be man handled. Mz. Becky Shepard / Grainger / Ford is accurate in her observation. That is correct, thank you young lady. Subjects not germain to these proceedings must be ignored, circumvented and dismissed outright. Twins? Oh dear. And this, this woman, your own mother... Oh my, are you alright my dear?

BECKY: Well It's none of your business and I am not your dear, but yes, all is well, my mother comes from money, yes, Those Grangers. My currently estranged soon to be ex husband is an artist, not an earner. He will love, and confuse his children. He has lost his amature status, he is saddled with a vain childish old woman who will die years ahead of him and he will realize he is gay soon, so yes, everything is just peachy. You don't pick your family as the saying goes.

THE INQUISITOR: ...So, in lieu of throwing up, I will defer to the standard procedural regimen for the liquidation of assets, liens, debts and estates such as these and leave it to the clerks and financial officials to do what they will... In closing may say I hope to never see or hear from a single one of you awful people again as long as I may live. *(he bangs the gavel, then crosses to a carnival mallet and unimpressively clubs the weight halfway to the gong, exiting with a sardonic "mic drop" discarding of the implement, duck faced.)*

(All the family gather in a tableau around the judges vacated throne as it transforms into a tombstone with the letters M. Sheppard. -yes, Death of a Salesman derivative- Thomas has one hand on Rebbie's shoulder and is holding Sheldon's hand with his other, Rebbie is caressing Becky's pregnant belly. Sam and Ruth are embracing and snogging crudely like teenagers. Sissy is cooking smack- preparing a tourniquet and shooting up. Marcus sits atop his own headstone with an overcoat rakishly draped over his shoulder, a Sinatra hat, a highball and a cigarette, still in corpse whiteface make-up.)

MARCUS: I never died.

THOMAS: You faked your own death?

MARCUS: Not explicitly.

REBBIE: I knew it.

BECKY: We all knew it.

THOMAS: Not me.

BECKY: All the women knew.

SHELDON: I knew.

SAM: We know.

THOMAS: Yeah, I guess I'm not surprised, but what happened that night, I thought you said he must have drowned Sam?

SAM: How would I know, I was drunk. I assumed. I haven't had a drink since. The pompous bastered ruined booze for me, it's lost it's kick.I thought he must've drowned, I dunno... Tom. Have I mentioned that you are a punk.

THOMAS: Yes you have.

SAM: And a weasel.

THOMAS: Yeah, you made that clear, I understand that violence is forthcoming.

RUTH: He's fucking your child's mother, that's something.

SAM: Violence is forthcoming, never fear.

SISSY: So gay... Da, I got a tattoo, it's a japanese octopus eating out a geisha girl and she has a tattoo on her thigh that says Shelby in New Times Roman.

MARCUS: Lovely. I had to escape. I just swam, I went under the water and swam to the bottom, through the black ink, into the silty bottom, I stayed under for minutes upon minutes, I surfaced a mile downstream of the raft and took a quick gulp and submarined again and again all night long, in the morning I floated on my back as the tide took me out past point lookout, past point no point, right on out into the shipping channel, I swam and swam, for days to the mouth of the bay, past Virginia Beach, beyond, I rounded the Del-Mar-Va peninsula. I caught flying fish and drank rain and lived on air and foam. I swam to the Emerald Isle and found my Shelby.

SAM: How could that be Marcus.

MARCUS: Magic.

SISSY: Did you really find Shelby Da?

MARCUS: I did.

SISSY: Was she all you'd hoped? Did you live happily ever after with your child bride? Did she save you?

SAM: Yes, Sissy, I found Shelby O'Brien, outside of Cork.

RUTH: Of course not Sophia, she would be 35 years old.

SAM: She was 33, she was married and had kids of her own, she was fat and unhappy and didn't remember me. She smoked while she nursed her wee bairn. I hated myself for longing after her, for finding her, I hated looking at her. I hated Ireland. I hated, hard.

SHELDON: That's nice.

REBBIE: Good.

SAM: Hardy-har.

RUTH: I'm glad.

MARCUS: Backatcha.

THOMAS: What's to become of us.

SISSY: We will die, everyone.

MARCUS: Can't happen soon enough.

BECKY: Hallelujah.

All 7 cast members aide Marcus as he prepares himself to perform ritualistic suicide. They speak this following wikipedia entry (<ins>https://en.wikipedia.org/wiki/Seppuku</ins>, retrieved 7/26/2015) facing upstage he eats, drinks, washes, dons the komono, etcetera, as the resplendent full moon rises and reveals itself from behind ominous clouds.

The following lines are divvied up among the cast, sometimes spoken in unison, overlapping and repeated, music and sounds accompany, it's a soundscape that crescendos early and tapers off towards a long plaintive denouement:

ENSEMBLE. Until this practice became more standardized during the 17th century, the ritual of seppuku was less formalized. In the 12th and 13th centuries, such as with the seppuku of Miyamoto no Yorimasa, the practice of a kaishakunin (idiomatically, his "second") had not yet emerged, thus the rite was considered far more painful. Seppuku's defining characteristic was plunging either the Tachi (longsword), Wakizashi (short sword) or Tanto (knife) into the gut and slicing the stomach horizontally. In the absence of a kaishakunin, the samurai would then remove the blade from his stomach, and stab himself in the throat, or fall (from a standing position) with the blade positioned against his heart.

During the Edo Period (1600–1867), carrying out seppuku came to involve a detailed ritual. This was usually performed in front of spectators if it was a planned seppuku, not one performed on a battlefield. A samurai was bathed, dressed in white robes, and served his favorite foods. When he had finished, his instrument was placed on his plate. Dressed ceremonially, with his sword placed in front of him and sometimes seated on special clothes, the warrior would prepare for death by writing a death poem.

With his selected attendant kaishakunin, standing by, he would open his kimono, take up his tantō or wakizashi —which the samurai held by the blade with a portion of cloth wrapped around so that it would not cut his hand and cause him to lose his grip—and plunge it into his abdomen, making a left-to-right cut. Prior to this, he would probably consume an important ceremonial drink of sake.

He would also give his attendant a cup meant for sake. The kaishakunin would then perform *kaishaku,* a cut in which the warrior was decapitated. The maneuver should be done in the manners of *dakikubi* (literally. "embraced head"), in which way a slight band of flesh is left attaching the head to the body, so that it can be hung in front as if embraced. Because of the precision necessary for such a maneuver, the second was a skilled swordsman. The principal and the kaishakunin agreed in advance when the latter was to make his cut. Usually dakikubi would occur as soon as the dagger was plunged into the abdomen. The process became so highly ritualised that as soon as the samurai reached for his blade the kaishakunin would strike. Eventually even the blade became unnecessary and the samurai could reach for something symbolic like a fan and this would trigger the killing stroke from his second. The fan was likely used when the samurai was too old to use the blade or in situations where it was too dangerous to give him a weapon.

This elaborate ritual evolved after seppuku had ceased being mainly a battlefield or wartime practice and became a para-judicial institution.

The second was usually, but not always, a friend. If a defeated warrior had fought honourably and well, an opponent who wanted to salute his bravery would volunteer to act as his second.

(lights bump out just before the mortal blow, a 2 second count and then in the pre curtain call dark a loud extended crash box sound cue, as if a restaurant wire shelving unit full of pots and pans and dishes and silverware was pushed down a flight of steps by a disgruntled dishwasher.)

An energetic curtain call with loud upbeat music and triumphant crosses and sweeping arm gesticulating, deep bows and curtsies and running leaping exits.

END OF PLAY

AUTHOR

Permission and royalty licensing must be directly arranged with the playwright for all public performances where admission is charged and / or the performance is advertised. Distribution of film, video, audio and other media reproductions of this fictional dramatic script requires special permission. No charge for classes, workshops, one time free performances and for actors using this material for auditions. Interesting low budget urban theater troupes will be accommodated 'cause I love you guys, please write me directly. If you are making or spending any money using this script I should get some.

C.M. Brophy copyright 2015 1st edition Brophy Amalgamated Publishing rhodeislandreds@gmail.com **4703 Banner, St. Hyattsville, MD. 20781 U.S.A**.

Made in the USA
Monee, IL
12 September 2025

24539981R00044